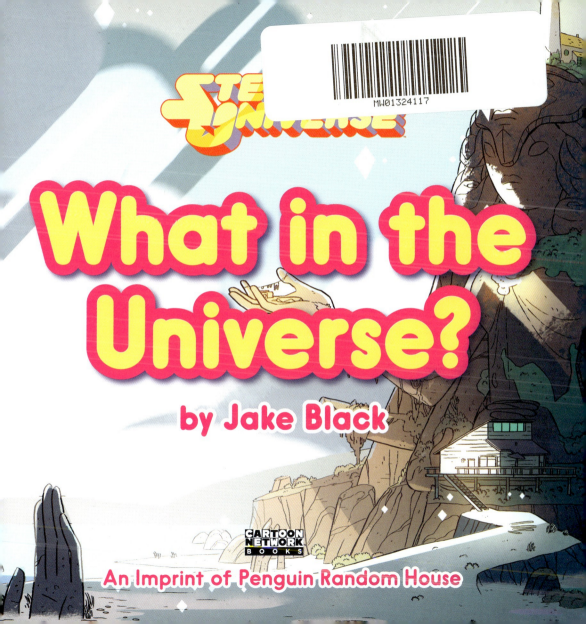

CARTOON NETWORK BOOKS
Penguin Young Readers Group
An Imprint of Penguin Random House LLC

Penguin supports copyright. Copyright fuels creativity, encourages diverse voices, promotes free speech, and creates a vibrant culture. Thank you for buying an authorized edition of this book and for complying with copyright laws by not reproducing, scanning, or distributing any part of it in any form without permission. You are supporting writers and allowing Penguin to continue to publish books for every reader.

STEVEN UNIVERSE, CARTOON NETWORK, the logos and all related characters and elements are trademarks of and © Cartoon Network. (s16). All rights reserved. Published in 2016 by Cartoon Network Books, an imprint of Penguin Random House LLC. 345 Hudson Street, New York, New York 10014. Manufactured in China.

ISBN 978-0-8431-8348-1   10 9 8 7 6 5 4 3 2 1

Cookie Cats are the most delicious, scrumptious ice-cream sandwiches in the universe.

Steven's Gem is a rose quartz, which he inherited from his mother, Rose Quartz.

The Crystal Gems protect the people of Beach City from danger.

Being the mayor's son isn't all it's cracked up to be. **Buck Dewey** makes the most of it by hangin' with the cool kids.

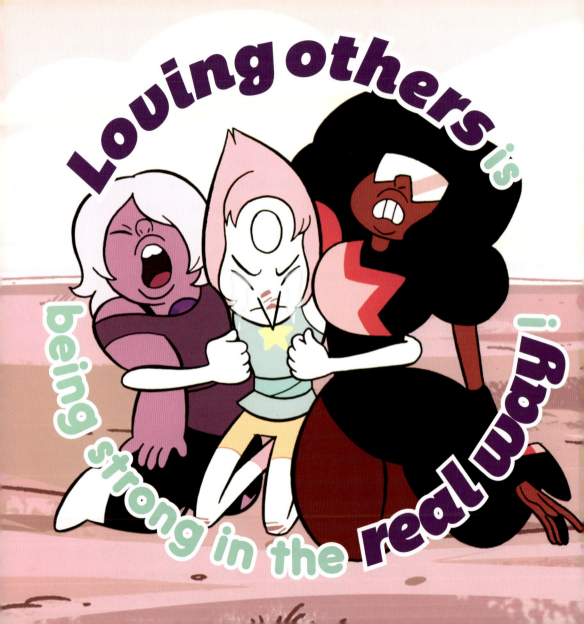

Sadie's mom packs her lunch every day. Sadie used to be embarrassed by that, but now she thinks it's pretty cool.

Lars is really good at making up excuses and pretending to be sick **so he doesn't have to go to work.**

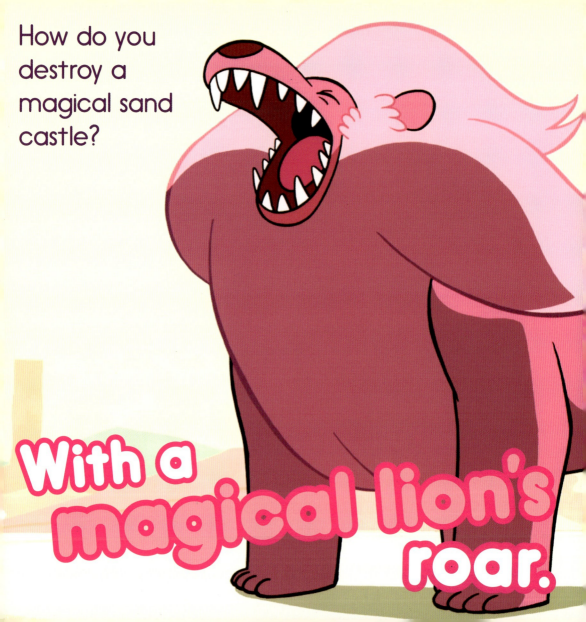

How can you fight what you can't see? No, seriously, I'm asking. How can you?

Because the Invisible Gem Monster is, well, invisible.

How can you fight it?

It's great to have
a fitness coach like
Steven to motivate you!

Steven dreamed he was playing chess with Dogcopter, the amazing movie hero who is a dog and a cop and a helicopter— all at the same time!

Even gems can get food poisoning if they eat something like this.

This is Rose Quartz's manifesto:

Fight for all life on the planet Earth. Defend all human beings, even the ones that you don't understand. Believe in love that is out of anyone's control. And then risk everything for it!

Garnet is actually a Fusion of two other Gems, **Ruby** and **Sapphire**, who love each other so much that they never wanted to be apart again.

Lions don't play fetch.

Or catch.

Or any games, really.

What do you do when the ocean dries up?

Go find the Gem responsible and make her put it back.

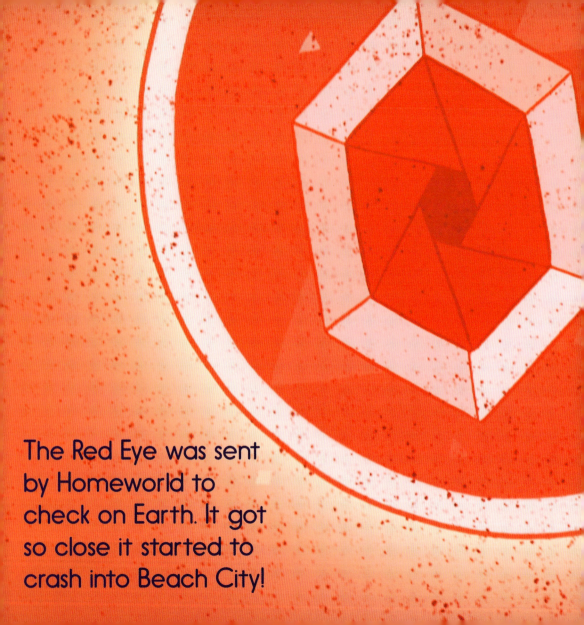

The Red Eye was sent by Homeworld to check on Earth. It got so close it started to crash into Beach City!

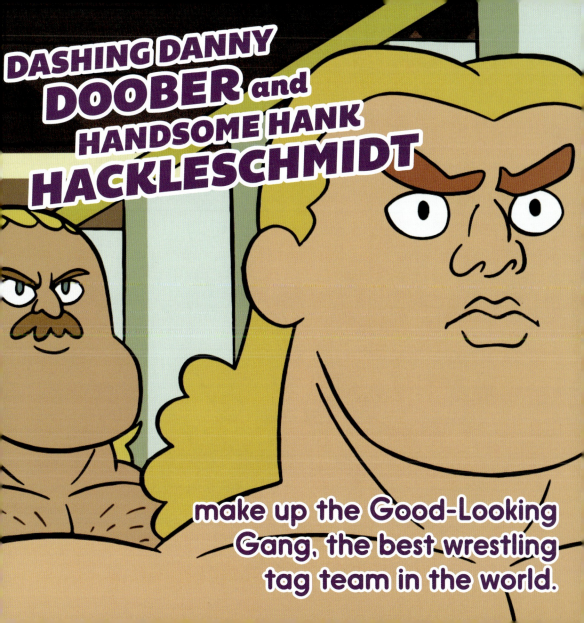

The Sky Spire is an awesome Gem temple. It's pretty much a spire in the sky.

Oh, and the Heaven Beetle lives there, too.

Going on a super-secret mission with your team?

You need a cool team name.

Like "SECRET TEAM"!

The Shooting Star is a rare and powerful elemental.

What do you do with it? Shoot it!

Seagulls are the worst. Seriously. The worst. Can you imagine anything worse than seagulls? **No. Because they are the worst.**

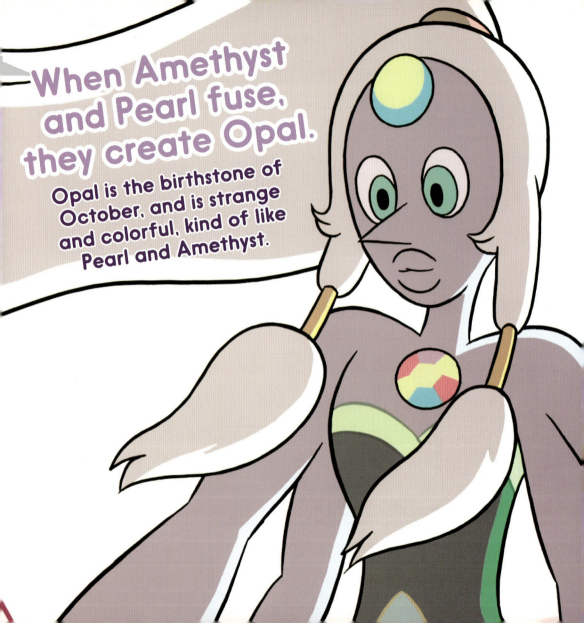

Can your
pet lion
walk on water
and teleport?

What? No? You don't
even have a pet lion?

Bubbles are super useful.

They can keep your friends and your lion and your dad and your dad's van safe.

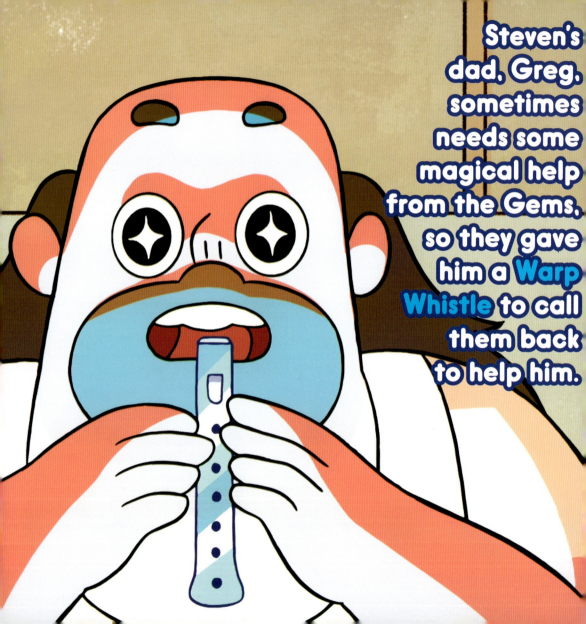

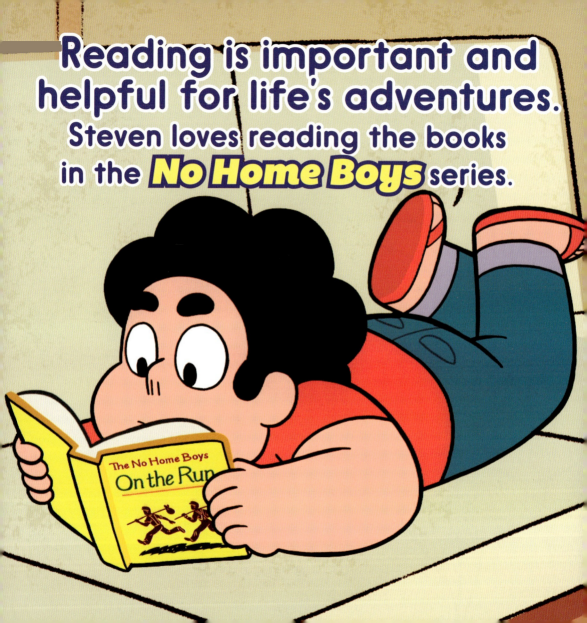

When Gems are corrupted, they become monsters. The Crystal Gems fight them.

Alexandrite the stone is a mysterious gem that seems to change its color.

Alexandrite the Fusion is a six-armed giant Gem. You don't want to get on her bad side.

These harmless-looking creatures are actually Drill Parasites that are tough enough to drill holes into the Temple.

There are few things creepier than a floating red eye that can destroy entire cities.

Families are awesome!

Steven's family may not seem like a traditional family, but at their core, they love and support one another—like families do.

Jenny and Kiki are twins, but they couldn't possibly be more different. Jenny likes hangin' out with her friends, while Kiki is always helpful around the family pizza shop.

Gem creatures take many shapes and forms,

including the form of a giant bird that can explode into smaller versions of itself.

The Desert Glass looks like a fancy pillow, but it can actually create walls and pillars just by being near sand.

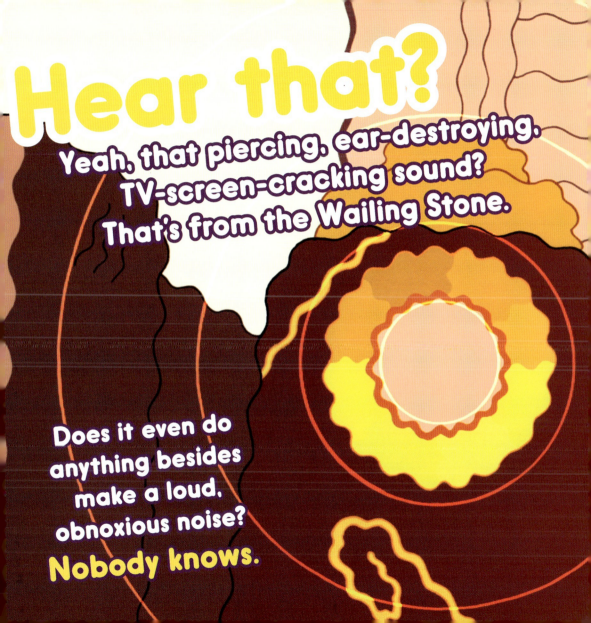

Connie is a good friend, and her tennis skills come in handy when learning how to wield a sword.

HIS BEST SONG IS

"Let Me Drive My Van (Into Your Heart)."

"I know I'm not that tall.

I know I'm not that smart.

But let me drive my van into your heart.

Let me drive my van into your heart."

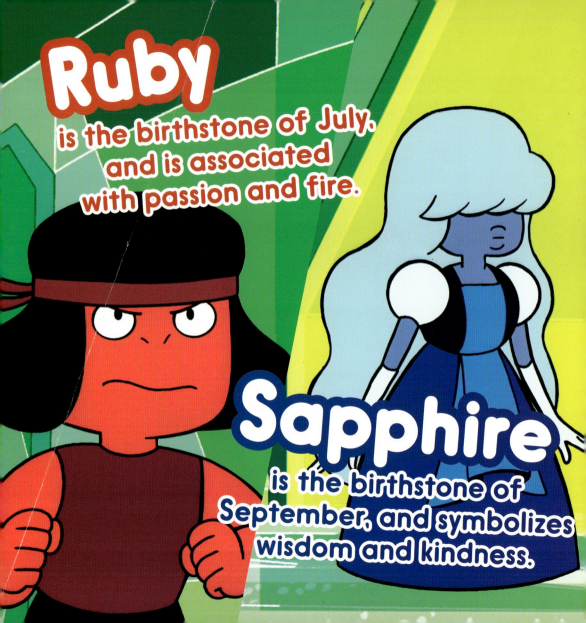

Want a quick way to look slick (or make up a good wrestling character)? Use margarine to make your hair look goooooood.

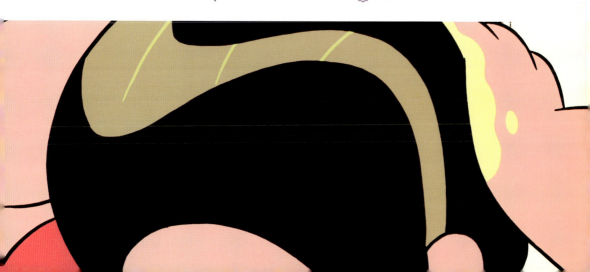

The old abandoned warehouse on the outskirts of town has many uses, including wrestling matches and teenage dance parties. Let's hope they never fix it up!

Peridot
is the birthstone of the month of August.

Some say it brings the wearer power and influence, but others say it should only be worn by people with clear, pure minds.

Connie used to need glasses, but Steven corrected her vision with his healing spit when Connie drank from a juice box that had some of his backwash in it. Gross, cool, or both?